Christmas Winterland

a colourful christmas adventure

Copyright © 2015 Christopher Mark Stokes

1

First edition published in 2015

All colouring images herein have been illustrated by the author and therefore may not be reproduced without the owner's permission.

Conditions of Sale

This book is sold subject to the condition that it shall not, by the way of trade or otherwise be lent, resold, hired out or otherwise circulated without the authors prior written consent in any form of binding or cover than which it is published.

www.christophermarkstokes.yolasite.com

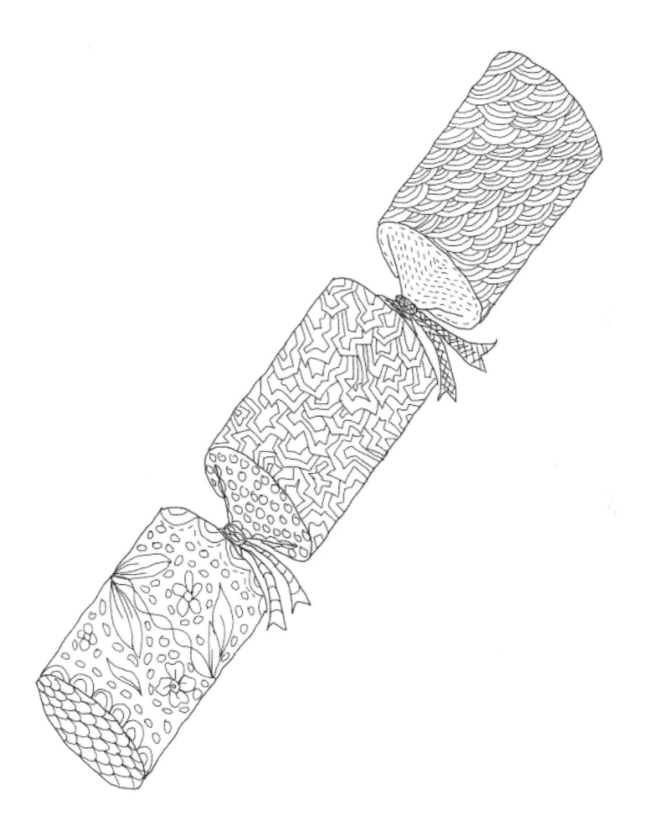

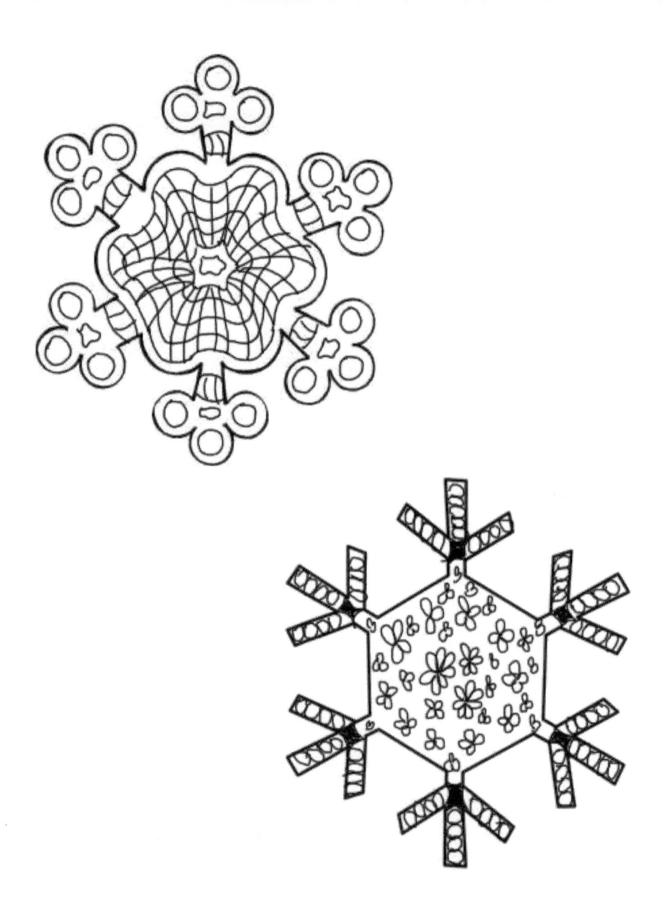

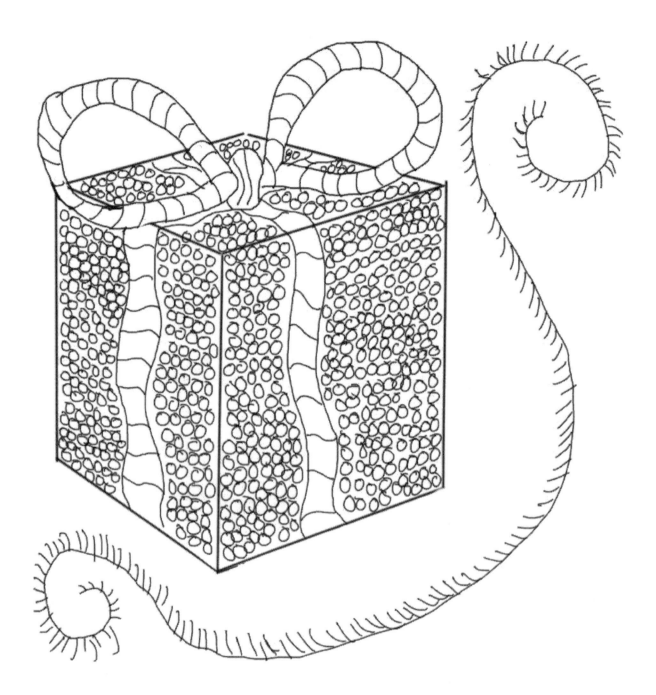

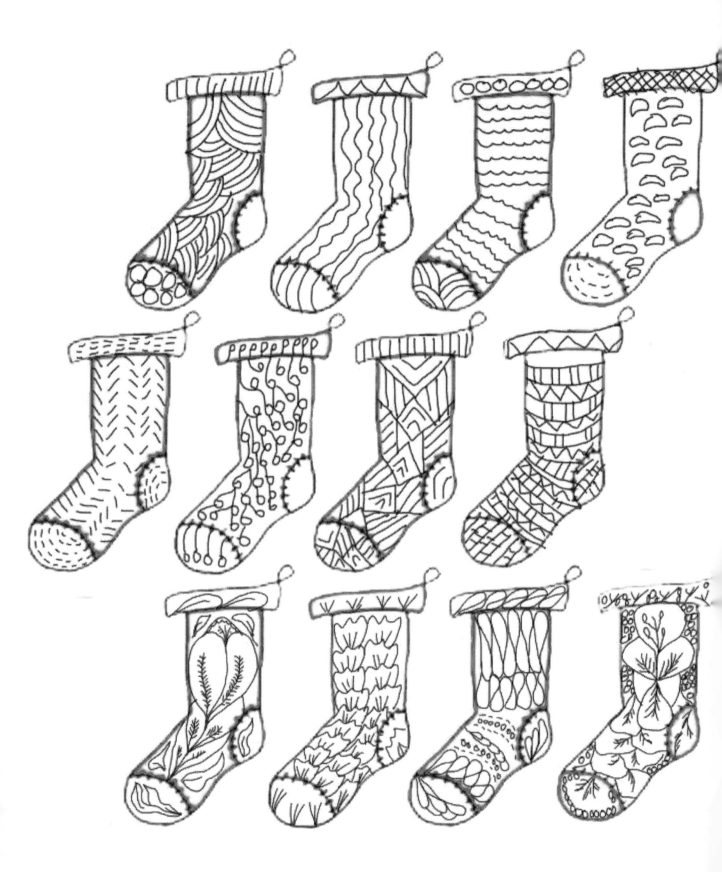

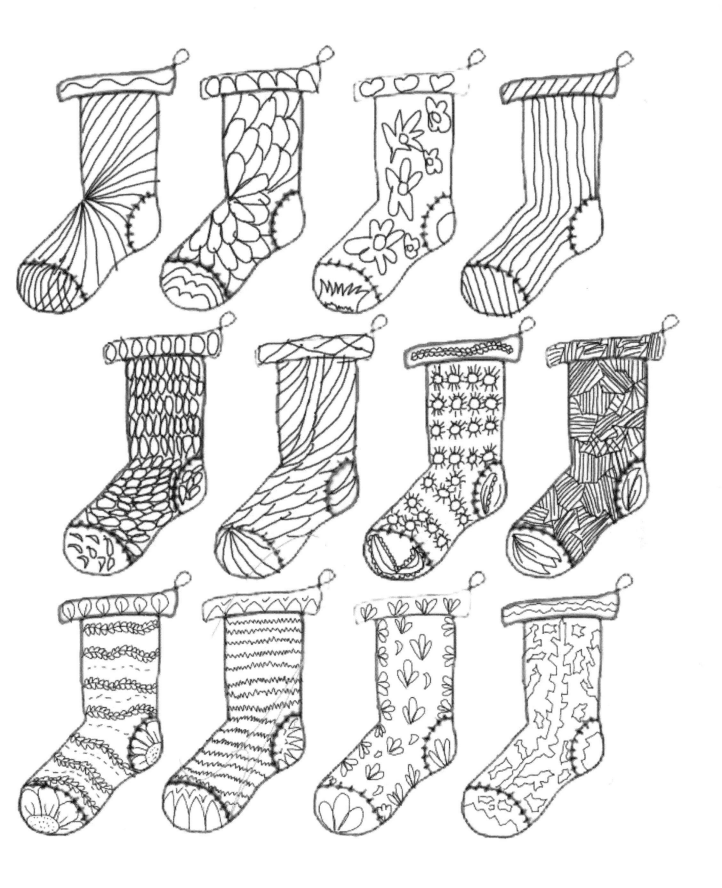

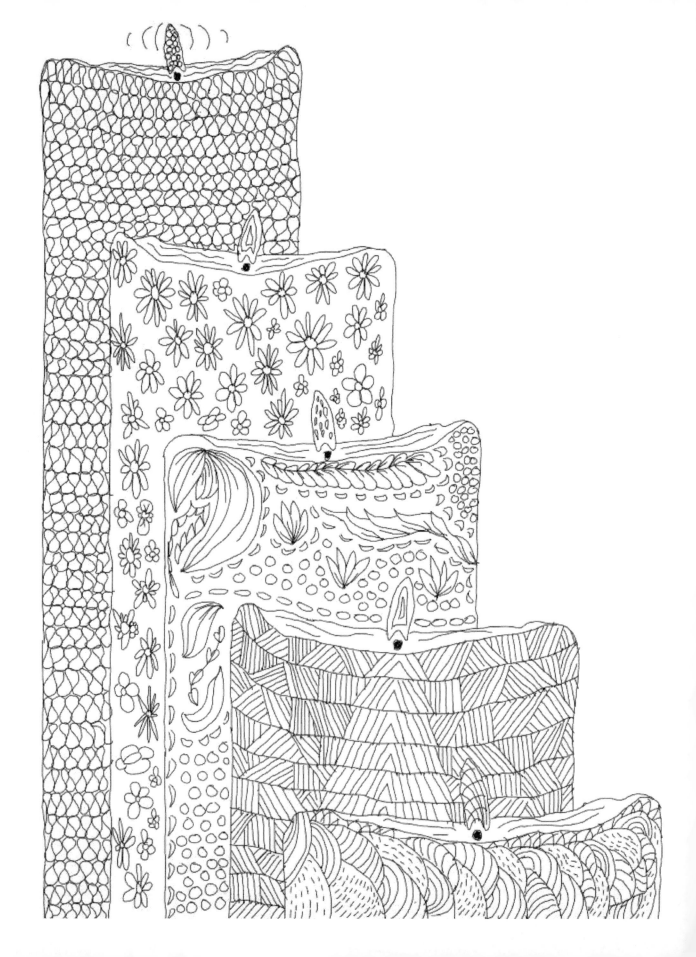

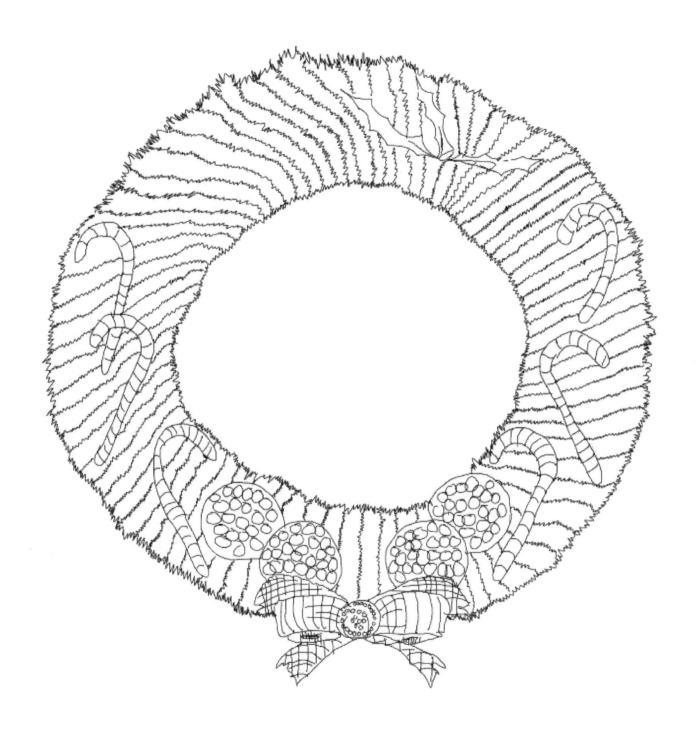

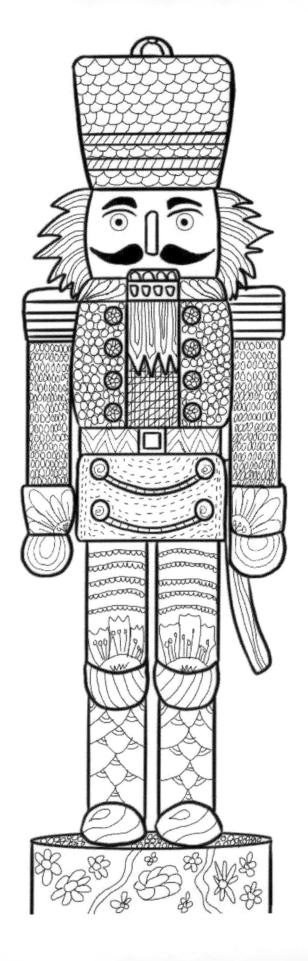

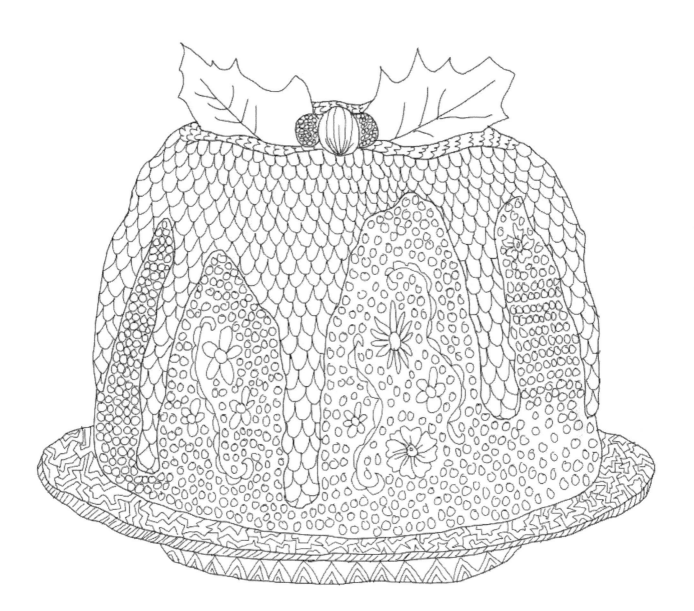

About the Artist

Christopher Mark Stokes was born on 8th January, and currently resides in Walsall in the West Midlands within the United Kingdom.
Already Christopher Mark Stokes has seen some of his books become bestsellers in various amazon categories, and with the constant support of his family he has written two novels; one in the fantasy genre and one in horror. Alongside these he has also written novellas and numerous short stories.

Christopher has also used his passion for art in order to create a plethora of illustrated children's books aimed at a variety of age groups; from two year old's to twelve year old's.

Christopher loves all things in relation to science fiction, fantasy and horror. Inspirations for his work are authors such as George R.R Martin, J.R.R Tolkien, Stephen King, Clive Barker and children's author Roald Dahl. He is also inspired by illustrator Quentin Blake.

Printed in Great Britain
by Amazon.co.uk, Ltd.,
Marston Gate.